DECISIONS DETERMINE DESTINY

ALSO FROM REVIVAL TODAY

Financial Overflow

Dominion Over Sickness and Disease

Boldly I Come

Twenty Secrets for an Unbreakable Marriage

How to Dominate in a Wicked Nation

Seven Wrong Relationships

Everything a Man Should Be

Understanding the World in Light of Bible Prophecy

Are You Going Through a Crisis?

The 20 Laws that Govern the Financial Anointing

35 Questions for Those Who Hate the Prosperity Gospel

The Art of Spiritual Warfare

Help for Your Darkest Time

Seven Reasons Your Church Will Never Have Revival

Who Told You You're in a Season of Waiting?

How to Prevail in Every Battle of Life

Decisions Determine Destiny

Books are available in EBOOK and PAPERBACK through your favorite online book retailer or by request from your local bookstore.

DECISIONS DETERMINE DESTINY

DEVELOPING A MILLION-DOLLAR DECISION-MAKING SYSTEM

JONATHAN SHUTTLESWORTH

Without limiting the rights under copyright(s) reserved below, no part of this publication may be reproduced, stored in or introduced into a retrieval system, or transmitted, in any form, or by any means (electronic, mechanical, photocopying, recording, or otherwise) without the prior permission of the publisher and the copyright owner.

The content of this book is provided "AS IS." The Publisher and the Author make no guarantees or warranties as to the accuracy, adequacy or completeness of or results to be obtained from using the content of this book, including any information that can be accessed through hyperlinks or otherwise, and expressly disclaim any warranty expressed or implied, including but not limited to implied warranties of merchantability or fitness for a particular purpose. This limitation of liability shall apply to any claim or cause whatsoever whether such claim or cause arises in contract, tort, or otherwise. In short, you, the reader, are responsible for your choices and the results they bring.

The scanning, uploading, and distributing of this book via the internet or via any other means without the permission of the publisher and copyright owner is illegal and punishable by law. Please purchase only authorized copies, and do not participate in or encourage piracy of copyrighted materials. Your support of the author's rights is appreciated.

Copyright © 2025 by Revival Today. All rights reserved.

Scripture quotations without attribution are taken from the Holy Bible, New Living Translation, copyright © 1996, 2004, 2015 by Tyndale House Foundation. Used by permission of Tyndale House Publishers, Inc., Carol Stream, Illinois 60188. All rights reserved.

Scripture quotations marked (KJV) are from the King James Version of the Bible, which is public domain.

April 2025
ISBN: 978-1-64457-665-6

Rise UP Publications
www.riseUPpublications.com

CONTENTS

Introduction — 7

Part I
DEVELOP A DECISION-MAKING STRATEGY

Strategy 1 — 15
Understand Mistakes Are Costly

Strategy 2 — 21
Does the Bible Specifically Address Your Decision?

Strategy 3 — 23
Make Your Decisions in God's Presence

Strategy 4 — 25
Don't Change Your Mind When You Leave God's Presence

Strategy 5 — 29
Listen to People Who Have What You're Trying to Get

Strategy 6 — 35
Make Decisions Based on Principles, Not on Emotions

Strategy 7 — 41
Make Decisions Based on Long-Term Success Instead of Short-Term Comfort

Strategy 8 — 45
Mentally Travel Down the Road of Your Decision

Strategy 9 — 49
Consider Potential Consequences and the Reactions of Your Enemies

Part II
SIX DECISIONS THAT CHANGED MY FUTURE

Decision 1 — 63
Aligning My Ministry with People Moving in the Same Direction

Decision 2 — 69
Preaching and Laying Hands on the Sick during COVID

Decision 3   75
Launching Check the News

Decision 4   81
Attaching Myself to Dr. Rodney Howard-Browne during COVID

Decision 5   85
Joining Dr. Rodney Howard-Browne at The Stand

Decision 6   89
Making Mistakes Moving Forward, Not Backward

Afterword   93
Author Photo   98
About the Author   100

INTRODUCTION

> My children, listen when your father corrects
> you. Pay attention and learn good judgment.
>
> — PROVERBS 4:1

Pay attention and learn good judgment. This is a necessary command from the Word of God. Decision-making is not a strength for most Christians. It sounds better to claim you have a generational curse than to admit you make poor decisions, but often that's the culprit. It's easier to blame a generational curse and seek spiritual intervention than it is to make better decisions.

> For I am giving you good guidance. Don't turn
> away from my instructions. For I, too, was
> once my father's son, tenderly loved as my
> mother's only child. My father taught me,
> "Take my words to heart. Follow my

> commands, and you will live. Get wisdom; develop good judgment. Don't forget my words or turn away from them. Don't turn your back on wisdom, for she will protect you. Love her, and she will guard you. Getting wisdom is the wisest thing you can do! And whatever else you do, develop good judgment. If you prize wisdom, she will make you great. Embrace her, and she will honor you."
>
> — PROVERBS 4:2-8

The Bible says the wisest thing you can do is get wisdom. So why is so little value placed on seeking wisdom and applying good decision-making?

The Bible promises that valuing wisdom will make you great. I don't understand how so many people write themselves off by claiming they don't know how to do things. Why don't you know? We don't live in 1100 AD. Knowledge and wisdom aren't stored in the Library of Alexandria under lock and key. It's easier to access information today than ever before.

I've been asked how to file paperwork to become a minister. Seriously? Look it up. It's mind-boggling when people message me questions like, "I saw you're scheduled to preach in Annapolis, Maryland. Where is that?" I often fight the urge to respond by saying: "You're on the internet. Type the question you asked me into a search engine, and the answer will magically appear."

INTRODUCTION

 There's no reason to be in the dark on any subject.

The Bible states that wisdom is the principal thing and compels you to get wisdom and understanding in everything you seek. So, go after it and get it, especially in the area of your calling. What are you setting out to do? You should read every pertinent thing you can get your hands on.

My friend, Taylan Michael said, "Formal education will make you a living. Self-education will make you a fortune." That's true, and he's proved it.

> "She will place a lovely wreath on your head; she will present you with a beautiful crown." My child, listen to me and do as I say, and you will have a long, good life. I will teach you wisdom's ways and lead you in straight paths.
>
> — PROVERBS 4:9-11

 You can walk in straight paths.

Your life should be a straight path. It shouldn't look like art school for a year and a half, then Bible college, then a home heating sales job. Stay in one lane and reject anything that doesn't coincide with the direction you're moving.

I titled this book *Decisions Determine Destiny* because Christians get confused about who's responsible for their outcomes in life. It's not God's sovereignty, it's not the Devil, it's your decisions that determine your destiny.

 Your life is a product of the decisions you make.

If you don't like where you are in life, change your decision-making system. Stop waiting for a better day. Make different decisions from today.

The Bible tells stories of people who decided to disobey the Lord and then died the same day. I could decide to go out drinking tonight. If I step into the Devil's kingdom for a bit, I think he has enough pent-up aggression and rage toward me to ensure I'm never seen or heard from again.

People die every day. I don't know how people can claim it's always possible to recover. If that's true, why do graveyards exist? The people buried there didn't recover. Things don't always work out in the end. I don't say this to be morbid, but I want you to understand that this happens because most people have never learned how to make good decisions.

Many people grow up without a father in the home. Some were raised by single mothers who struggled to make sound decisions because it's difficult to function well alone. Many people, even in two-parent homes, were never taught good decision-making while growing up. This book will teach you how to make good decisions that will create and save you millions of dollars and keep you from making costly mistakes.

PART I
DEVELOP A DECISION-MAKING STRATEGY

STRATEGY 1

UNDERSTAND MISTAKES ARE COSTLY

When you walk, you won't be held back; when
you run, you won't stumble.

— PROVERBS 4:12

I don't know how anyone can read Proverbs 4:12 and develop a theology that claims we all make mistakes. The Bible says you can walk in wisdom and not be held back. Biblical wisdom enables you to run without stumbling. You don't *need* to make mistakes. In 1 Kings 13, God used a prophet to perform mighty signs and wonders, which impressed the king.

> Then the king said to the man of God, "Come to the palace with me and have something to eat, and I will give you a gift." But the man of God says to the king, "Even if you gave me half of everything you own, I would not go with you. I would not eat or drink

anything in this place. For the Lord gave me this command: 'You must not eat or drink anything while you are there, and do not return to Judah by the same way you came.'" So he left Bethel and went home another way. As it happened, there was an old prophet living in Bethel, and his sons came home and told him what the man of God had done in Bethel that day. They also told their father what the man had said to the king. The old prophet asks them, "Which way did he go?" So they showed their father which road the man of God had taken. "Quick, saddle the donkey," the old man says. So they saddled the donkey for him, and he mounted it. Then he rode after the man of God and found him sitting under a great tree. The old prophet asks him, "Are you the man of God who came from Judah?" "Yes, I am," he replies. Then he says to the man of God, "Come home with me and eat some food." "No, I cannot," he replies. "I am not allowed to eat or drink anything here in this place. For the Lord gave me this command: 'You must not eat or drink anything while you are there, and do not return to Judah by the same way you came.'" But the old prophet answers, "I am a prophet, too, just as you are. And an angel gave me this command from the Lord: 'Bring him home with you so he can have something to eat and drink.'" But the old man was lying to him.

— 1 KINGS 13:7-18

The decision to listen to a command from the Lord over the word of some guy who claimed he heard from an angel should not require much thought. It's an easy call, especially when a stranger claims to have been told you're to do the opposite of what the Lord commanded you to do, but the man of God in this passage of Scripture didn't listen.

> So they went back together, and the man of God ate and drank at the prophet's home. Then while they were sitting at the table, a command from the Lord came to the old prophet. He cries out to the man of God from Judah, "This is what the Lord says: You have defied the word of the Lord and have disobeyed the command the Lord your God gave you. You came back to this place and ate and drank where he told you not to eat or drink. Because of this, your body will not be buried in the grave of your ancestors." After the man of God had finished eating and drinking, the old prophet saddled his own donkey for him, and the man of God started off again. But as he was traveling along, a lion came out and killed him. His body lay there on the road,

> with the donkey and the lion standing beside it.
>
> — 1 KINGS 13:19-24

There are some mistakes you can recover from quickly at a low cost and some mistakes you can recover from after a long time at a great cost, but there are other mistakes you can never recover from.

The man in this story was a prophet used mightily by God, but his track record didn't override his poor decision. You never become so anointed that you can make poor decisions without consequence. That's not how life works. God's hand may have been on your life thus far, but you decide how long it continues.

Jonah was a prophet so mightily anointed he turned an entire city-state to God in less than forty days with one sermon. But when he was on a boat headed in the wrong direction and away from God's will, he was more cursed than the heathen on the boat with him.

That's why I abhor any teaching that makes people comfortable with mistakes. Preachers will get up and say things like, "How many know He's the God of the second chance, and third chance, and fourth chance?" and be met with applause. I don't want that many chances; I want to get it right. Contrary to what other preachers might say, there are some mistakes you can't recover from.

My goal is to avoid making any mistakes. Mistakes are costly. You'll never value a decision-making system if you think everything always works out or that God is a God of unlimited mercy. Don't fall in love with the mercy side of God; fall in love with the instructions of God. Yes, God is merciful, but it's not wise to live your life solely by His mercy.

STRATEGY 2

DOES THE BIBLE SPECIFICALLY ADDRESS YOUR DECISION?

When you're faced with a decision, ask yourself: Does the Bible specifically address my situation? If it does, no further debate or reading is required. Do what the Bible tells you to do. The Bible explicitly addresses many things. It provides instructions for choosing a spouse, conducting yourself in marriage, raising your children, leading as a pastor, and a myriad of other specific situations. Paul wrote to Timothy and gave him sixteen scriptural qualifications for pastors.

You don't need to ask yourself or other members of your family if you should tithe. What is there to decide? The Bible tells you exactly what to do. Living in rebellion against God's Word under the guise of "thinking it over" isn't fooling anyone. Very few people will come right out and say, "I've decided to rebel against God." They attempt to disguise it as something noble. They claim they're thinking it over, planning it out, or praying about it. If the Bible specifically addresses the decision you're making, do what the Bible says. It's that simple.

STRATEGY 3

MAKE YOUR DECISIONS IN GOD'S PRESENCE

When I preach, I often blurt out an instruction, new direction, or undertaking. When the Spirit of God comes upon me, I know what to do, and I speak it at that very moment because the direction is crystal clear to me. You can enter God's presence in services, worshipping the Lord with anointed music, all-night prayer, or any time you decide to press in.

Even more than that, you can spend time in His Word to know Him better, and you will hear His voice more clearly. If you draw near to God, He will draw near to you (James 4:8). God can speak at any time between 12 a.m. and 11:59 p.m., and you can receive direction from God for an aspect of your life. However, you're not likely to hear from God by spending time in godless places, doing godless things (Proverbs 28:9).

STRATEGY 4

DON'T CHANGE YOUR MIND WHEN YOU LEAVE GOD'S PRESENCE

Consider the conversation we read in 1 Kings 13:

"The Lord told me not to eat and to go home a different way."

"No, you can have something to eat," said the old prophet.

"Okay."

You'll always have an opportunity to retreat from God's instruction, but don't do it. Things are exciting when they're new, but when the excitement wears off, and the reality of the expenses and work associated with the instruction sets in, people often abandon ship. Most people lose their excitement for a new idea after a week or so once they understand the true cost and realize the amount of work involved.

People have proclaimed they would move to Pittsburgh to attend Revival Today Church. Many followed through. Others didn't; they lost their excitement once they started looking up U-Hauls and apartments in the area and backed away from a decision they made under the anointing. That's why the prophet was killed in 1 Kings 13. I'm not implying you're going to die if you don't move to Pittsburgh; it's simply an illustration.

As a young evangelist, I often experienced situations where we'd have a great meeting, and the senior pastor would invite me to preach on Sunday morning and again on Sunday night. Then they'd ask me if I was available to come back for a full week because they felt it was something their church needed. I'd give them a week or so to call and schedule it before following up. Too many times to count, a pastor who initiated a conversation about having me in for a week of revival meetings changed his tune quickly after he was no longer flowing in the anointing. I'd often hear things like, "I was just looking at our calendar, and we have a Royal Rangers outing, then summer camp for the teens, and then in July, most families are away on vacation. So, we really can't fit a week of revival meetings in our schedule this year." The Lord spoke to their spirit, but they allowed their flesh to override it.

> **Your spirit has veto power over your flesh, but your flesh does not have veto power over your spirit.**

The moment God speaks to you and gives you instructions, the only thing you should allow your mind to think about is *how* to accomplish it, not *whether* you should accomplish it. Your mind should not be used to check your spirit. Your mind is a vehicle that enables you to reach the destination given to your spirit. Use your mind to think about the best way to accomplish what the Lord has given you to do.

Anytime God gives you an instruction that seems like a daunting or overwhelming task, break it down into bite-sized pieces so it becomes more manageable. If the Lord spoke to you to write a book, break it down into accomplishable steps. Don't view it as one big task; look at it as several small tasks to be completed in order. When the Lord speaks to you to do something, stay the course. Don't waver.

STRATEGY 5

LISTEN TO PEOPLE WHO HAVE WHAT YOU'RE TRYING TO GET

Where no counsel is, the people fall: but in the multitude of counselors there is safety.

— PROVERBS 11:14 (KJV)

A lack of counselors guarantees a fall. Too many preachers claim we all fall, but I want you to understand that is incorrect—you don't have to fall. The Bible shows you how to walk without falling (Jude 1:24-25).

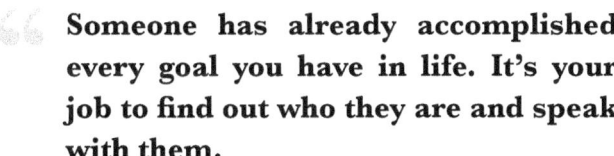 **Someone has already accomplished every goal you have in life. It's your job to find out who they are and speak with them.**

Listen to people who have what you're trying to get. Rodney Howard-Browne has already accomplished all that I aspire to do in evangelism, so I talked to him about how I could achieve my goals in ministry. It's not like the old days when a pastor could tell his congregation to attend an event, and the whole church showed up in full force.

How do you handle situations that require you to build a crowd? I asked Pastor Rodney how to hold a crusade, especially without churches backing you. He showed me how to host a successful crusade with a sizeable crowd when not even the local churches can draw a crowd. He also explained what to do when several churches claim their support for your crusade but end up backing out and leaving you with one pastor and a deacon.

Listen more than you talk.

The Scriptures tell us to be quick to listen and slow to speak (James 1:19). When you approach people for their advice, don't tell them what you've done; ask them about what they've done. Learn how to seek advice and listen. You don't need to share your testimony with people who haven't asked. If you're the one seeking advice, don't be the one who's always talking. Listen. You don't know what you don't know, and you don't know what they know, so listen to them.

I'm not suggesting that myself and others don't want to hear your testimony. I enjoy hearing testimonies of what God's done, but don't approach people offering to tell them everything God's done in your life since the time you were seven years old. Please don't force your testimony on people.

Seek legitimate council.

The Bible says in the multitude of counselors there is safety. Many years ago, Dake wrote in his notes, "Safety, providing they are really counselors."[1] He must have felt then like I feel now. I strongly suggest you listen to those who have done what you're trying to do. I also recommend you don't listen to anyone who *hasn't* done what you're trying to do. If your unemployed mother tries to discourage you from starting your own business, just nod your head and go about your business. If your mom has used public transportation her whole life and tries to discourage you from owning a car, don't listen to her, either. Talk to people who have done what you're trying to do, not those who have never even attempted it and prefer to discourage others from moving forward. Not everyone is a counselor. Everyone has opinions, but opinions are not valid counsel.

 Not everyone is a hater.

People are willing to help you learn what you don't know, but you have to diligently seek them out (Matthew 7:7-8). Before our ministry owned a jet, we chartered private aircraft. While we were still chartering, two people asked me why I wanted to own a plane when I could charter them as needed. I didn't have the answer

---

1. Dake, F. (2014). *Dake's Annotated Reference Bible: The holy bible, containing the old and new testaments of the authorized or king james version text*. Dake Publishing, Inc.

to the question, but I knew someone who would. I asked Jesse Duplantis about the advantages of owning an aircraft. I knew he wasn't going to respond by saying, "I never thought about it. In fact, I'm just going to sell my plane and start chartering." I knew he'd have the answer I needed. In forty-five minutes, he gave me four great reasons why owning an aircraft is better than chartering one. When you ask the right people the right questions, you gain wisdom.

Jesse also told me he would talk more about buying aircraft with me when I was ready. He offered to put me in contact with his mechanics once I needed one. It pays to speak with people who have done what you're trying to do. If you're unsure what to do in an area of your life, it's proof you haven't talked to someone who's already done it—it's your fault.

I don't have to remain in the dark on any subject.

If there's ever a time you're confused about anything, there's someone who can show you what to do. The medical field catalogs everything they learn, but in Christianity, most people don't record the blueprint God has given them for their gifts and callings (Exodus 25:8-9, 40). This is one of the frustrating flaws of Christianity in times past, but today you can overcome it.

Who ran Brother R.W. Schambach's tent crusades? I don't know, and whoever it was has probably passed away—we can never ask them to share their knowledge.

No instructions from his crusades are written in any book—I don't understand why that is. When Billy Graham's crusade director, Dr. James Coldiron, passed away, everything he knew about holding crusades died with him. Thankfully, I had the chance to talk with him when I was in my twenties.

I'm writing this book to share valuable insights I've gained throughout my life. I realize that not everyone has had the chance to talk to the same people I have.

Everything God wanted us to know is in His Word. He wrote a book and made it available for anyone to read. That's how it should be. Wisdom shouldn't remain a secret. Holding information in secret is cult-like behavior. It's what the Freemasons do. You don't need to reach the twenty-third level of Christianity before I'll share truths with you.

STRATEGY 6

MAKE DECISIONS BASED ON PRINCIPLES, NOT ON EMOTIONS

How someone feels about what you're doing should have no bearing on your decision, and if you're an adult, that includes your parents. Make decisions based on principles, not based on the reactions of others.

I've heard ministers claim to believe in healing, but they wouldn't dare preach about it at their church because it would upset members of their congregation. Some preachers reference a minister with a healing ministry who fell into sin in the 1970s, as if that's an excuse to steer clear of divine healing. Who cares? If this mirrors your thought process, you're not a good decision-maker. A good decision-maker does what's right, not what makes people feel comfortable.

> **Do what's right, not what makes people feel comfortable.**

I'm often asked how I get away with what I do in ministry. What am I getting away with? I'm not committing felonies or misdemeanors. I don't get away with anything. We don't take opinion polls in our ministry. Seeking the approval of others is a great way to live in a self-imposed prison. If I wanted my church to have optimal sound on Sunday mornings, I wouldn't poll the audience to see who thought last week's service was too loud and who felt it wasn't loud enough. I'd hire a sound engineer to analyze the sound and implement what they suggest. That way, I'm guaranteed to have the best sound. Don't change course based on the opinions of others.

Most pastors are scared to do and say anything on Sunday mornings without first asking if it's okay with everyone.

"We're going to serve communion right now, is that all right?"

"We're going to stand to worship, is that okay?"

"If you're comfortable, we ask you to clap your hands."

Don't allow yourself to be a prisoner to people's opinions your whole life, and don't be concerned about what makes people comfortable. Do things the way you know they need to be done. Don't live your whole life out of the will of God because your mother would be upset if you moved. You have one life, my friend; live it the way God shows you, regardless of what others around you think.

Comedian Jerry Seinfeld once asked David Letterman for advice after being offered a show by NBC. Letterman advised, "If you're going to fail, fail *your* way." He knew NBC executives would provide notes and suggestions to improve Jerry's show, but these executives weren't comedians. They'd never made anyone laugh; what did they know about comedy? Letterman's message to Seinfeld was clear: "If you listen to those guys, they'll ruin your show. Do it your way. If you get canceled, it will be because of your own decisions. You'll know it was because you weren't funny or that America didn't like you, but don't get canceled by listening to people who want to turn you into something you're not." Jerry Seinfeld listened to Letterman's advice. He and Larry David ignored NBC's suggestions and created a unique television show that people try to copy to this day. Do it your way. Otherwise, you'll turn into a vanilla replica of everyone else.

If you follow me on social media, which I don't recommend, you've likely read something that made you laugh. The same comment that made you laugh, upset other people and they unfollowed me, but why should I deprive you of laughter because someone else doesn't think I'm funny? If you don't think I'm funny or feel offended, follow somebody else; there's no shortage of ministers. I enjoy making people laugh; that's why I do it.

What would happen if I listened to my critics? If I stopped doing everything that people criticize me for, what would be left? Imagine if I stopped joking, decided not to preach hard and loud, and quit teaching on prosperity and healing. There'd be no reason for my existence as a preacher. I wouldn't be anointed or funny. I'd be a manila folder glued to a beige wall and easily replaced by some other minister who isn't funny or anointed. Don't allow people's opinions to drive you to irrelevancy. You'll end up being voted out and replaced at the drop of a hat.

Be who God made you. If I were a normal pastor, I would've turned Adalis into a loser. I would have insisted she stop flailing her arms and corrected her speaking style until she turned into every other woman on Christian television. Most people allow their critics to define them. Jesus never allowed His critics to define Him. He executed His mission and paid more attention to those who received His ministry than to those who didn't.

I'd venture to say that most ministers have made their ministry a prison. They don't enjoy being at their church, and they don't enjoy preaching at their church because they've allowed their critics to put them in a box. Most preachers can't even let a joke hang for one second without apologizing. I'm referring to ministers worried about offending people in America—not Iran. They won't be shot if someone finds their joke offensive. An angry email delivered to your inbox is the worst thing that can happen.

That brings me to another important point. You need to have a gatekeeping system in your life. The only emails that get through to me are testimonies and compliments.

You should have a similar protection system. Someone once came to me and apologized for an email they wrote a year ago. He was going through a rough time, and he didn't like something I said. I responded truthfully and told him not to worry because I never saw it. Nothing reaches me unless it's encouraging because I have a gatekeeping system. Few people should have access to your phone number or email. Have you ever heard me say, "I need to be careful here to avoid getting a lot of emails?" I don't receive those emails. Giving people unchecked access to you will negatively impact your mind.

Years ago, I downloaded an app that tracks who unfollows and follows me on Instagram each day. On the first day, I woke up and checked it and saw eight people had unfollowed me. One of them was an assistant pastor at a church where I preach from time to time. I couldn't help but wonder, 'What's his problem?' I knew right then I needed to delete the app. I didn't want to begin each day by fixating on who my posts might have offended the day before. It wouldn't have taken long before it ended up affecting how I preached. You can tell when people lack a gatekeeping system because they constantly talk about people who dislike what they're doing.

STRATEGY 7

MAKE DECISIONS BASED ON LONG-TERM SUCCESS INSTEAD OF SHORT-TERM COMFORT

Almost every pastor who closed their church during COVID held the same beliefs as Pastor Rodney and me. We all faced harsh criticism on social media and received nasty messages and even death threats. As a result, many church leaders discovered they could make all the unpleasantries disappear by shutting down their churches. They made decisions based on their desire to eliminate immediate pain and discomfort rather than focusing on the long-term. It's always better to endure short-term discomfort and even harsh persecution for long-term success.

> **Endure short-term discomfort for long-term success.**

By applying this principle, our ministry experienced significant financial growth. We went from $3.1 million in 2020, before COVID, to $15.2 million in 2021. This success came after enduring over 400 death threats, a negative local CBS News interview, and a critical article in the Pittsburgh Post-Gazette that deemed me a dangerous minister. That was a particularly rough two-week period, but it led to an incredible four years of progress and growth. Interestingly, the Pittsburgh Post-Gazette no longer employs the journalist who wrote the hit piece, and the reporter from the CBS interview was demoted before resigning.

Be prepared to deal with short-term problems to gain long-term success. Don't compromise to make challenges disappear. Many pastors who criticized the actions leading to Pastor Rodney's arrest in Florida wish they were the ones arrested. Where are the people who warned that an arrest would ruin his ministry? Most have had to lay off a significant portion of their staff and are struggling to rebuild, while Pastor Rodney's ministry is thriving. He made decisions based on principle. He was willing to endure short-term discomfort for long-term success.

Our ministry decided against accepting the PPP loan offered to churches by the government. At the time, we weren't seeing anywhere near the kind of money coming in as we do today. We could have really used it. Patrick, our CFO, reasoned that accepting government funds might not be such a bad idea with President Donald Trump in office. Ultimately, we decided against it, and as it turned out, President Trump did not stay in office, and the federal government had the power to retroactively use the acceptance of those loans to control the finances of every ministry that took the funding.

It's wise to focus on long-term goals over short-term reactions. Don't be swayed by the fluctuating feelings and emotions of others. *"Mark out a straight path for your feet, then stay on the path and stay safe"* (Proverbs 4:26).

STRATEGY 8

MENTALLY TRAVEL DOWN THE ROAD OF YOUR DECISION

Think about how your decisions will play out. This is an important step to take before making decisions; always consider the results of your actions.

"Jonathan, my wife and I quit our jobs to have more time to pray. We haven't been able to pay our bills."

That's because you never allowed your mind to travel down the road of your decision before you made it. I'm no economist, but if you cut off all your income, chances are you'll be broke within forty days.

Another thing to consider is the reactions you'll face because of your decision. People think I have a quick wit, but my responses on X or in the comments section of Instagram aren't made on impulse. I anticipate what people might say and have my responses ready. It's like having ammunition preloaded in a gun, ready to fire. The key is to stay ahead of others' reactions.

Camila asked me how to handle a problem with a classmate. I asked her to describe the person she was dealing with and show me a picture. Then, I told her what to expect. "When they say this to you, be ready with this response." Then promised her that the person would never bother her again. Think ahead, anticipate how others will react, and leave them astonished by your preparedness.

If you've ever been laid off at work, you probably should have seen it coming. There are usually signs—your boss starts treating you differently, or the budget is cut for the third time this year. You should monitor the financial health of your employer. Have they had a good year or a terrible year? Are there rumors of layoffs? When these changes happen, you should already have a plan for what you will do. Think ahead. Don't be a reactionary Christian. Be proactive.

While growing up, my favorite ice hockey defenseman was Ulf Samuelsson from Sweden. He was known for his hard hits, and he lived by the motto: "*Initiate, don't retaliate.*" If someone hit him, he wouldn't slash him back and end up with a penalty. He was always the one to strike first, then his opponent would retaliate and get the penalty, leaving him doubly mad because he got hit and ended up with a penalty, too.

Be the person who causes the reaction, not the person who reacts to what's happening around them. It doesn't matter what any administration is planning. Those in government should be more concerned with what I'm preparing to do. I don't spend my time reacting to the latest news. I stay informed of the facts, but my life is driven by my goals and the path God's given me, not by what people are doing around me. Nothing can alter that.

STRATEGY 9

CONSIDER POTENTIAL CONSEQUENCES AND THE REACTIONS OF YOUR ENEMIES

Ask yourself this question: 'If I was the Devil, how would I attack me?' Once you identify your vulnerabilities, put buffers between you and the potential attack.

When we first moved into our building on Patton Drive, I asked Patrick if we had a signed agreement with the owner allowing us to use his parking lot. When he told me we didn't, I knew what needed to be done because if I were the Devil, I'd find a way to offend the parking lot owner so they'd revoke their verbal agreement. I instructed Patrick to put a plan in place in case he changed his mind. I knew we needed to be prepared, and the Devil attacked exactly how I knew he would. They backed out of our agreement, but we were prepared. The Devil has no new tricks—his attacks are easy to anticipate.

> So that Satan will not outsmart us. For we are familiar with his evil schemes.
>
> — 2 CORINTHIANS 2:11

You can outsmart the Devil; he isn't the smartest character.

 You can outsmart the Devil.

How many shootings must happen before every pastor implements a plan to protect their people? Having several members of your church who carry weapons is not a plan. If thirty-five people stand up and start firing away, it'll end in disaster. It would be best to have a plan that discourages shootings from happening.

When you arrive at The River Church in Tampa, Florida, there's a police car sitting at the entrance. During *The Stand*, the church's mass healing and miracle services, there was a police sniper on the roof of the church at the ready. The plan Dr. Rodney implemented greatly discouraged anyone planning to give the church a problem. It's called getting ahead of the problem.

When we held an outdoor crusade in Pennsylvania, my father warned me that people would call in noise complaints. He instructed me to have the permit officer write the decibel level limit on the permit. He knew they'd say it didn't matter, but he explained I should make them give me a number and have a decibel meter available. That way, when the police respond to a

DECISIONS DETERMINE DESTINY

complaint, I could show them I complied with my permit.

Exactly what my dad warned of happened. When we went to get the permit for the outdoor crusade, we requested the maximum decibel level be put in writing on the permit. Just as my father said, they claimed it wasn't necessary because the park was used for concerts all the time, and they never had any complaints. We insisted, and they recorded a limit of ninety-one decibels on our permit. Sure enough, while I was preaching, the police arrived in response to numerous noise complaints. We showed them our permit, pointed to the decibel limit, showed them the noise level on the meter we kept by our sound booth, and they left satisfied.

America has freedom of speech. The only legal way the Devil could have shut us down was with noise complaints. If we hadn't expected the problem and taken the necessary steps to address it, the police would have insisted we lowered our volume. There's no doubt they'd come back and tell us to turn it down again and again until our sound was off. Thankfully, God has given each of us a brain capable of thinking and anticipating problems so we can defend against the attacks of the Devil.

Another common attack of the enemy is false accusations. We've anticipated this as well. It's impossible to molest someone at our church because there are cameras and security personnel everywhere. We set up the children's room in a way that prevents people from entering at will. Security personnel patrol the area. A local prison warden monitors the security feeds from all our cameras and has trained others on how to do it. If someone looks shady, there's a member of our security team on them right away.

The Devil also loves to attack finances. That's why we have protocols to ensure no one steals our money. I read a news story about a church that lost $750,000 to an email wire transfer scam. Internet hackers intercepted their email transaction and posed as the person they were wiring money to for their church building. When you wire money, it's gone. It's not like a credit card transaction; it can't be reversed by anyone. The church started a GoFundMe to recuperate their money, but even if they get it back, they've lost credibility. You can recover from it, but it's a mistake with serious consequences.

What safeguards do you have in place in the realm of health and safety, finances, and legal matters? Those are the three main areas the Devil seeks to attack.

THREE QUESTIONS TO ASK YOURSELF

1. What health and safety protocols do I have in place?

I've already explained the safety protocols we've implemented in our ministry and church, but I've applied personal protocols to protect my family as well.

I bought my wife an SUV because I don't want my daughter riding around in a compact sedan that could end up totaled if they were hit by a 12-speed bicycle. If a lady changed lanes without looking and hit my wife's SUV, the impact would total her car and leave Adalis' SUV with minor scratches or dents. I'm not in control of the vehicle choices of others, but I am in charge of my wife, and I will take care of her.

2. What financial safeguards do I have in place?

Very few people can routinely handle money without giving in to the temptation to steal it—believing otherwise is foolish. I assume the temptation could arise even within people I trust, so I've set up protective systems. It's not about suspicion; it's about recognizing the truth about human nature and acting wisely to protect assets and people.

An older businessman once asked me about the safeguards I had in place to ensure no one stole money from our ministry, and I had to admit I wasn't sure. When I asked Patrick, I found out that to steal money from our ministry, my wife, my wife's sister, Magalis, and Patrick all have to sign off on it. If my wife turns against me, it's over, anyway.

If you're a pastor, do you have the same two people count the offering every Sunday? That's not a smart plan. It's not difficult for two people to agree to steal money. You need at least nine people, three teams of three, to count money. You should regularly alter the rotation. It's easy to conspire with one person to steal. It's difficult to get nine people to commit a crime together, and if, for some reason, you have nine thieves in your church, you need more Holy Ghost meetings!

One of the worst lies we teach people in church is to give people the benefit of the doubt and trust people without question. A teenager could tell his dad he thinks there's something off with the youth pastor and be rebuked for it. "How dare you say that about him? He went to Bible school." When you're not allowed to question if something is wrong, people could end up molested or worse. I'm not suggesting it's permissible to make false accusations or malign people in front of others, but the Bible teaches that we're not even supposed to trust ourselves, let alone other people. You should trust no one but God and His Word.

I believe anyone could do anything. I watched an episode of *Forensic Files* from the 1990s where two couples met at a nightclub, and they went back to a condo in Maryland. The host couple locked the doors, drew a gun on their guests, forced them to undress, and shot them. Then, after the girlfriend cleaned up the crime scene, she walked in on her boyfriend in the bathtub with the severed heads of their victims floating beside him. The couple was later convicted and received a thirty-year prison sentence, which seemed lenient to me. Then it hit me: the episode aired in the '90s, which means the couple received parole in 2018. If there's a guy who took a bath with two severed heads walking the streets, it means there are demon-possessed psychopaths among us. Keep that in mind as you're loading groceries into your car.

I don't mention that to put fear in you. *"God has not given us a spirit of fear, but a spirit of love, power, and a sound mind"* (2 Timothy 1:7). You can know these harsh realities without needing Valium, but you should have a realistic understanding of the world you live in. Look around before you load your groceries into your trunk. Don't be another victim, abducted while coming out of a mall, or shot, or robbed. Be vigilant and use safeguards (1 Peter 5:8). I take this very seriously.

One time, I was walking into a Nordstrom in Pittsburgh. I had just parked my Cadillac in the back of the lot when a man in a sweatshirt with his hood up passed by me, and then abruptly turned to follow me. That didn't sit right with me. I turned and looked him directly in the eyes and he became defensive and said, "What?" "I'm just checking what you're doing," I replied. He seemed offended that I thought he might be a robber, but if I was wrong and he wasn't a robber, I lost nothing by being cautious. Ignoring my instincts for the sake of political correctness could have cost me my belongings or my life. Political correctness will get you killed.

If I were walking in downtown Philadelphia and two guys in hoodies turned around and started walking behind me, I'm going to assume they are coming to kill me. If I'm wrong, praise the Lord, but if I'm right, at least I gave myself a heads-up. I'm willing to die for the Gospel, but you'll have to earn it.

Most of you reading this haven't been taught these realities in church. People think everyone is a "good guy" with a "good heart." That's great—tell his cardiologist. I love people. I'm very relaxed, but I refuse to allow American Christianity to turn me into an idiot.

There was a church shooting in Texas a few years ago. The shooter entered through the main doors of the church dressed in a ski mask, black tactical gear, and carrying a backpack. When I first heard the story, I assumed the killer entered through a side door and just opened fire. Not even close. After walking in through the main entrance, he walked down the center aisle to the front row, turned around, took the gun out of his backpack, and started shooting while the pastor ignored it and continued preaching.

Religious Christianity trains you to ignore everything and just hope the Lord works it out. The Lord will not work it out. The Lord put *you* here to work it out. You're the authority; God put you in charge. The Great Shepherd doesn't take care of the sheep; the under-shepherd is charged with taking care of the sheep.

According to Psalm 91, the blood of Jesus covers you, but the blood of Jesus is not a substitute for wisdom. My daughter, Camila, is covered by the blood of Jesus, but I'm not giving her the keys to my car to drive to school. Nothing should surprise you. People are capable of anything.

Judas was not demon-possessed when Jesus made him a disciple. Later, a demon entered Judas. Just like someone can be bad when you meet them, and the Lord can change them, someone can be good when you meet them, and later, the Devil can change them. Patrick doesn't steal money now, and he may not be tempted to either, but blind trust is foolish.

The Bible tells of mighty men of God with major miracle ministries who fell into destructive sin. People can change. I've heard pastors criticize churches with armed security, but every time there's a problem, churches call the police to have them take care of it. Meanwhile, the shooter runs out of ammo killing everyone while leadership waits for the police to show up. If something goes wrong, you'll be forced to act. Why not decide to act ahead of time and have a plan in place?

3. What legal safeguards do I have in place?

You're likely to face some type of legal challenge if you live in America. I'm not worried about Islamic Jihadists barging into my church and attacking me. Not today, not in Pittsburgh, Fort Worth, or even Los Angeles. There are always people looking for a reason to sue you, your ministry, or your business. That's why we have catchers in all our meetings. Sometimes, people get in line to fall so they can claim they hurt their neck and sue the church. One minister was sued by someone who tried the same scheme at six other churches. His church won the case, but it cost time and money.

Another legal area that often trips people up is taxes. Make sure your taxes are in order. Anyone can count money and create spreadsheets. I've told Patrick that his primary job is to keep me out of jail for financial impropriety. This is not a call to live in fear, but you must proactively place buffers everywhere the enemy might attack.

> **Your mind is capable of outthinking the Devil, human enemies, and any potential problems.**

There will always be obstacles, but you can outthink these hurdles. Paul said, *"For a wide door of opportunity for effectual [service] has opened to me [there, a great and promising one], and [there are] many adversaries"* (1 Corinthians 16:9). You have the mind of Christ, so use it. You're not under a generational curse, you just make poor decisions. You can change, make good decisions, and teach your children to do the same.

> **God gave you a brain so you could give Him a break.**

Not everything requires prayer and a miracle. Most of the time, correct thinking neutralizes the need for supernatural help. Seek miracles when needed, but don't rely on them for simple things you can sit and think through beforehand.

A major difference between a wealthy home and an apartment is that apartments don't have a room called a study; wealthy homes do. Wealthy homes have a place where a man can sit in peace and think. When I met Jimmy Swaggart, he had two Bibles and a notepad in front of him. At eighty years old, he still sat at his desk alone to study and think. Learn to think. God gave you a brain so that you could give Him a break. From the beginning, He put Adam in charge of the Garden of Eden. He doesn't want to be dragged into every event.

PART II
SIX DECISIONS THAT CHANGED MY FUTURE

DECISION 1

ALIGNING MY MINISTRY WITH PEOPLE MOVING IN THE SAME DIRECTION

I received my license as a minister with the Assemblies of God at nineteen years old while attending Bible school. According to their bylaws, the licensing requirement was three years of Bible college.

I was happily affiliated with the Assemblies of God from 2000 to 2007. I didn't have a problem with the Assemblies of God, but our relationship ended when they closed the National Office of the Evangelist. I wrote them a letter to turn in my credentials, and they called to ask me to write another letter that explained why I was leaving. In my original letter, I thanked them for licensing me at such a young age. I acknowledged that most of my preaching opportunities had come from Assemblies of God churches. I wasn't leaving on bad terms. The Assemblies of God decided to support pastors, youth pastors, missionaries, and worship leaders and remove evangelism. I didn't leave because I was upset; I left because God called me to be an evangelist.

It didn't make sense to continue a path with an organization that didn't align with my values.

Although the Assemblies of God may prioritize aspects of ministry differently today, back then, their focus was predominantly on supporting pastors, missionaries, youth pastors, and worship leaders. There wasn't even an option to minor in evangelism at their Bible colleges.

The general superintendent met with a minister I know and shared his view on evangelists. He mentioned that when he was a pastor, he never felt the need to invite evangelists to his church. He believed his staff could take on anything an evangelist could do. That's how he felt about evangelists, and he's entitled to feel that way.

Leaving the Assemblies of God was a pivotal decision. If you're familiar with Pastor Rodney Howard-Browne, you might know he doesn't like when people say, "Go where you're celebrated, not where you're tolerated." I understand what he means when he says that, and I agree with him, but breaking company with the Assemblies of God was a decision to prioritize the call of God on my life and avoid a situation that would most likely lead to strife.

When we held our crusade in Asbury Park, New Jersey, we faced numerous death threats, serious enough to warrant support from the Department of Homeland Security. They deemed the threats credible and acted to ensure our safety as we proceeded with the event. It was a spiritual battle we had to endure to complete the task God gave me, but it would have been foolish of me to move my office headquarters from Pittsburgh to New Jersey in the middle of a city that was threatening my life just to prove a point. In Acts 4, when Peter and John were freed from prison, they returned to their own company. You shouldn't live your life in a continuous state of spiritual warfare.

I left the Assemblies of God, not with bitterness but with a positive outlook. I made a conscious decision to detach myself from them and join those who honor and appreciate the office of the evangelist. In doing so, I didn't have to combat people who had harsh things to say about what God called me to do. People who'd say things like, "These evangelists blow in, blow up, and blow out. They take all the church's money with them, and you'll never see them again." People are free to feel how they want, but the Bible says in Amos 3:3, *"How can two walk together unless they agree?"*

My decision was twofold: I decided to leave without becoming a bitter minister who left their denomination. I also decided against becoming a bitter minister who stayed in their denomination. There are people in the Assemblies of God who have nothing good to say about the Assemblies of God; they sound like idiots when they accuse their denomination of backsliding while still being under them. You shouldn't be part of something you badmouth.

After leaving the Assemblies of God, God opened the door and knit me to Revival Ministries International Ministerial Association and Pastor Rodney. He is an evangelist who celebrates evangelism. Once I made that move, my ministry changed.

The pastors who are part of RMIMA welcome evangelists. They often invite evangelists to their churches to preach. It was a nice change of pace from the stares and crossed arms I was used to receiving.

My point isn't that ministers should leave the Assemblies of God. It illustrates a choice I made to break out of my comfort zone and away from the company of familiar people, practices, and places to go to the next level. Not everyone from your past can come with you to your future. There's a natural, fleshly desire in people to bring along every childhood friend and family member as they pursue the path God has for them.

The Bible shows that it's rare for people to keep their nuclear family unit intact throughout their lifetimes. I don't mean divorce—although many people struggle with that, too. Jacob had twelve sons, and within a generation, the cousins were physically attacking each other in hand-to-hand combat and burning cities to the ground.

Have you ever witnessed the patriarch of a wealthy family acquire a large plot of land to build homes for his children? Thirty years later, one son marries a woman who hates his brother, and they end up selling their house and moving to another state. Maintaining a close-knit family throughout generations is very difficult. People can't even keep their own families together. There's no way you can successfully take a large group of friends and extended family forward as you pursue God's call for your life.

Anytime you make a move in life, the people who were with you on the last level are often the ones who fight you the hardest over moving to the next level. You must become comfortable with letting go and be willing to do what God has called you to do. If people support you, wonderful, and if people don't support you, it's not a problem. They don't see what you see, and you don't have to convince them.

DECISION 2

PREACHING AND LAYING HANDS ON THE SICK DURING COVID

The decision to continue preaching in person and laying hands on the sick during COVID was the defining decision of my life up to this point. I'm leaving out starting Revival Today Church because that wasn't my decision; I was just doing what the Lord told me.

During COVID, we received over 400 death threats in three days, and the local news and newspaper ran a hit piece. I could have made it all go away if I'd remained virtual, but I continued to do what God called me to do. I understood Facebook and YouTube algorithms enough to know that unsaved people wouldn't see my online broadcast unless it went viral; they only showed it to Christians. Social media platforms know which of their subscribers are Christians, and they even know what type of Christian content they prefer. Our content doesn't typically reach reformed Christians who hate the healing and prosperity message.

At the time, deciding to continue preaching in person seemed like a certain death, but hundreds, if not thousands of people discovered my ministry through *Check the News*. A former Mormon found me on *Check the News*, liked the show, and came to one of my services in January of 2021, where he gave his life to the Lord. Now, he's a member of our church and a volunteer for our ministry. That wouldn't have happened if we went one hundred percent online.

When I decided to stay open, the only person, friend, or associate I heard from was Pastor Rodney. Once the news coverage of me aired, I didn't hear from anyone in my family except my mother. People distanced themselves—and I don't mean social distancing. No one wanted to be associated with a lunatic who was intent on preaching during COVID. There was an upfront cost to pay for staying open during COVID. Close friends of ours sent out emails to a large list of people stating their disagreement with our decision and assuring people that we were no longer welcome at their church. Success has an upfront cost and a long-term reward, and safety has an upfront reward and a long-term decline. We could have kept all our old friends and continued talking to people on the phone.

My news interview with KDKA is an example. If you were to read the comments from the first few months after it aired, everyone called me a lunatic. They said I was going to kill people and demanded I be put in prison for attempted murder. But if you keep scrolling to read the comments posted five or six months later, they were all people asking where our church was located. Don't base your decision on what's popular because people's opinions change all the time. Any pastor who shut their church down in March of 2020 was considered a hero and celebrated by the media, but today, if that's the route you took, your ministry is in trouble.

Decisions determine your credibility. You're not a credible minister if you preached healing for fifteen years and as soon as a disease came, you compromised. Either the name of Jesus has authority all the time or not at all. They cut their legs out from under everything they'd ever preached. If you preach on a subject, you have a responsibility to move forward and ride it out if you want to remain credible. A healing minister who shuts down his ministry during a pandemic is the same as a prosperity preacher who stops tithing during a financial crisis. You gain credibility with people when you live what you preach.

During COVID, ministries still received money even though they shut down. Many people are committed tithers and givers. Ministries realized they could shut down without taking a financial hit in the short term, so they did.

I wasn't a pastor when COVID hit. Financially, I didn't need to stay open to stay afloat. I had planned a vacation to Arizona that I was very much looking forward to, but I felt as a spiritual leader, it would have been irresponsible to go on vacation while so many people struggled. Instead of taking my vacation, I decided to host *Check the News* every night, teach during the day, and preach at churches until we received a reprieve. In May 2020, when President Trump deemed churches essential, it was like a fog lifted.

When people were worried and full of fear, some even suicidal, I decided to stand with people. I wasn't worried. I had money. I had a job. I'm self-employed. I can't get fired. I decided to stay with the people, mostly through a screen, but I wasn't going to broadcast on YouTube about recipes to make while you're home with the kids during quarantine. I wanted to offer something that would help people.

Our ministry has experienced a 12-fold increase since the decision to stay open, and it continues to grow. People were looking for someone who could use the Bible to address what was happening in the world, and they couldn't find anybody. Most ministers were airing repeats or listing off fun games to play at home with the kids during quarantine. People were freaked out, and they had questions. Were we in the tribulation? Was this the rise of the Antichrist? The mark of the beast? What did the Bible have to say? I decided not to back down or wait a year to fight, and it changed the trajectory of our ministry.

I'm not attempting to write an autobiography. I'm taking you through the decisions I've made, highlighting the difficulty I faced in making them, and telling you what they've produced.

Hindsight is twenty-twenty. Everyone knows it was the right decision to make now, but at the time, even I wondered.

DECISION 3

LAUNCHING CHECK THE NEWS

At the time we started *Check the News*, I'd been doing a daily 10:30 a.m. teaching broadcast on YouTube. While flying from Connecticut back to Pittsburgh after the lockdown had been announced, the Lord told me people were scared to death. He revealed that when I did the 10:30 a.m. broadcasts, I dealt with people's spirits. I read Psalm 91 to them and told them about the protection and healing power of God, and although they believed me, their minds were still full of fear and worry. He told me to deal with their spirits during the day and their minds at night. So, I started by telling them about the infection fatality rate.

Most people don't remember this, but leaders like Gavin Newsom in California predicted there would be 26 million COVID infections and 1.2 million deaths in California alone. One pundit on MSNBC and CNBC predicted that by May 8, 2020, every hospital bed in the

United States would be full, and people would have to treat their loved ones at home with palliative care.

Then I discovered Yossi Gestetner, a Hasidic Jew from Brooklyn, and a data-driven strategist. He ran the numbers from the Diamond Princess cruise ship and concluded that COVID was either deadly and not very contagious, or contagious and not deadly, but not both. Based on the Diamond Princess case study from February 2020, not enough people died for COVID to be as deadly as what they were projecting.

Then I had another thought. If I were to broadcast on social media from my kitchen table using my phone, and claim the infection fatality rate wasn't really that high, and start referencing Yossi Gestetner, I'd look like a lunatic. But if I had a microphone and a quality camera, it would add to my credibility. I knew that a group called Right Wing Watch was monitoring me carefully. They were constantly editing clips of preachers who claimed COVID wasn't that bad. I decided to highlight tweets from experts instead of rambling on for an hour and a half and look like a nut with a video wall and a microphone.

I didn't speak my opinions; I gave people expert opinions. Some people didn't like them, some didn't agree with them, but I wasn't speaking my thoughts on COVID. I cited verified accounts and people like Dr. Scott Atlas from Stanford and Yossi Gestetner—men who aren't Christians. That dealt with people's minds in a way that even the professional preacher-mockers couldn't find fault with because I wasn't offering my opinion. It set people's minds at ease to know they have protection according to Psalm 91, and even in the natural, COVID was nothing to be worried about. The feedback from our audience was overwhelmingly positive. People put the broadcast on at night, and even though I was yelling, it helped them sleep.

When disturbing news broke that the state of Pennsylvania intended to hire 200,000 contact tracers to remove COVID-19-infected children from homes and hospitalize them, I showed it was logically impossible. The state government couldn't execute a 200,000-person hiring program if they had fifteen years to make it happen; it was way beyond their capability. If the same people responsible for operating the DMV were tasked with managing door-to-door vaccination, there was nothing to worry about. The government is not capable of that type of organization. There was no way they could have mobilized a 200,000-person workforce of contact tracers. When you present facts logically, it puts people's minds at ease.

There was talk of restricting interstate travel for the unvaccinated. How were they going to do that? There are too many roads. The government couldn't enforce that at the border of New Mexico to Arizona, let alone the entire country. Local and federal governments made scary-sounding threats, but once we examined them on *Check the News*, it was clear their threats were impossible to execute. We experienced a large increase in viewership, most of them are now permanent ministry partners and friends because we went through a type of Vietnam together.

I'm grateful for my wife. I give her credit. I'm sure many other ministers had to shut down because of pressure from their wives. When faced with death threats against their child, many women would have taken their kids and gone to live with their parents until the threats against their family stopped. Most women would have flipped out if they received a pair of little girls' underwear in the mail with their daughter's name on it and a note attached that read, "I'm going to kill you, prosperity preacher." These were not fake death threats—we turned the threats over to the FBI. Through it all, I never heard one word of complaint from Adalis.

I faced one major concern about doing *Check the News*. With all the Black Lives Matter riots and COVID concerns, I didn't have time to edit the cursing from the video clips. We were doing a religious broadcast from a religious ministry with more cursing than programs aired on HBO Max—there was filthy language every night. I wanted to obey the Lord, but there was no practical way to edit that many clips every day. I felt uneasy about playing a video of riots with nonstop foul language. I figured I'd lose about eighty percent of my partners. It was a significant risk, but I took the risk in obedience to what the Lord had directed me to accomplish. Most people didn't care. In fact, people seemed to enjoy the raw footage of those unafraid to say what they were thinking, even if they used harsh language. After listening to people threaten your life every day, it was somewhat therapeutic to hear people dish it right back.

When Rodney Howard-Browne was arrested, we had people iron his mugshot on black T-shirts and mail them out. The response was so overwhelming our ministry offices turned into a T-shirt sweatshop. It was hot around the clock from the number of Rodney Howard-Browne faces being steamed onto shirts. Later, a man who owned a T-shirt company volunteered to do all the T-shirts at cost. Amazing!

Check the News was a decision that changed our future. At the time, we had around eight people on staff, and now we have over sixty. That decision resulted in the growth of every aspect of our ministry.

DECISION 4

ATTACHING MYSELF TO DR. RODNEY HOWARD-BROWNE DURING COVID

Many ministers who were licensed and ordained through Dr. Rodney Howard-Browne turned their credentials in after he was arrested. They didn't want to be identified with him anymore. They feared staying connected with him would ruin their ministry and reputation. Most of their ministries are now half of what they once were. Rather than repent and make things right, they covered their bad decisions with a hundred more bad decisions.

The Bible says in Proverbs 16:18 that *"pride comes before destruction, a haughty spirit comes before the fall."* Pride won't allow you to admit and correct a mistake. It would have been wise to speak with Pastor Rodney and apologize for getting caught up in the COVID hysteria, admit they made a mistake, and haven't found another covering for their church since they left. They could have admitted Pastor Rodney made the right decision, acknowledged his ministry is four times what it was before he was arrested, and prayed he considered allowing them back into RMIMA, but they just continued down the road of bad decisions and watched their whole ministry go down the drain. When Pastor Rodney was arrested, he told me I was the only preacher who returned his text messages or phone calls. People run when trouble comes, and I never ran.

Anyone worried their ministries might suffer because of their affiliation with Rodney Howard-Browne would be better off understanding that their ministry faces greater scrutiny by simply aligning with the Bible. Not that your ministry is ruined in the eyes of Heaven—far from it, but in the eyes of the world, you are an anti-LGBT, right-wing, hateful bigot because you believe in the Bible. So, who cares? If your ministry ever grows to a notable size, you'll be interviewed and asked if you believe homosexuality is a sin. Then you'll have a choice to make. Your only options are to either stand firm on the Word or stammer around the question and gain the world's approval and lose God's. Why would a preacher attempt to make sure they have a "good name" anyway? Jesus said, *"They hated Me. How much more will they hate you?"* (John 15:18).

I took a stand and publicly supported Pastor Rodney; I wasn't content with offering quiet support over the phone. In stark contrast, another pastor my age criticized Pastor Rodney in a large chat group he had created to guide us through the challenges of COVID.

During the height of the Black Lives Matter demonstrations, a pastor in the Western United States dedicated a month-long sermon series to pro-Black Lives Matter topics like white privilege—a bold move for a white pastor. Pastor Rodney reached out to him with a warning that his decision would cripple his church because the movement was rooted in communism and socialism and had nothing to do with black lives. He pointed out that the founders of Black Lives Matter were practicing witches. He told the pastor that allowing this spirit into his church would ruin it. The pastor respectfully disagreed and moved forward with what he thought was right. In one month, he lost every single tithing member of his congregation and was forced to start from scratch—it could have been avoided if he listened.

The night Pastor Rodney was released from jail, I titled my broadcast, *They Arrested My Friend*, and it caught international attention. That was also when I announced our plans for a Woodstock-style Easter event. In the aftermath of that broadcast, I was met with silence from many fellow ministers. The ones I did hear from said things like, "They're only asking us to shut down for fifteen days bro, you're making a big mistake." However, Bishop Eristhee from St. Lucia messaged me. Given his background as an older Caribbean Black pastor, I assumed he would tell me I was nuts for taking my stance. Instead, his message was quite the opposite: "You showed yourself to be a true son of your spiritual father tonight. Good job." What kind of person bails on their spiritual father when he's under attack? If you can't stand with those whom you're knit to in the spirit, you're a loser.

One decision that will impact your success in life is choosing whom to listen to and whom to admire. You won't listen to someone you don't admire. When you admire someone, you don't argue with them—admiration causes you to keep your mouth shut and listen. The people you trust, listen to, and admire will greatly affect your success.

DECISION 5

JOINING DR. RODNEY HOWARD-BROWNE AT THE STAND

Pastor Rodney Howard-Browne was arrested in March 2020 for refusing to close his church. As a result, he initiated *The Stand*—a daily open-air gathering where people could gather to worship and hear the Word of God preached in defiance of illegal government overreach. *The Stand* underlined that nothing would stop the preaching of the truth of the Word of God, including government mandates.

Today, the decision to support *The Stand* seems like a no-brainer, but at the time, I planned to attend for one week, hug Pastor Rodney, congratulate him for getting out of prison and starting *The Stand*, attend the services, and head out. I had a full schedule of meetings booked for the year and intended to remain in my comfort zone. I was comfortable preaching at churches and receiving offerings.

Early on, there weren't many people attending *The Stand*. People wouldn't come on the buses from the inner city because of the curfew in place. There was no promise that any money would come in from the meetings. Pastor Rodney told me it would mean a lot to him if I stayed for the summer and preached at *The Stand* with him. I told him about all the meetings I had planned, and he just repeated, "It would mean a lot to me if you could do *The Stand* with me." When he said it the second time, I knew the Lord was speaking to me.

Many years ago, evangelist R. W. Schambach had heart-related issues that prevented him from holding a scheduled meeting in Chicago. He called my Uncle Ted and asked him to cancel his plans and preach the Chicago meeting for him. That may sound like an enormous opportunity, but not if you know how ministry works. When you hold a meeting like that, you're responsible for the money to finance it. It's not a big payday; it's an enormous expense.

The Lord reminded me of how my Uncle Ted helped his spiritual father, Evangelist Schambach, and he told me, "Now it's your turn. He's just gone through a lot. He needs you around. He'd like you around. Serve your spiritual father."

I rented a short-term three-month lease condo and moved to Tampa with Adalis and Camila. I continued to host *Check the News* from my phone after the meetings. There were no more than three hundred people spread out on that massive field. *The Stand* was an aggressive move. It looked like I would help Pastor Rodney at a massive loss. He never promised to pay me or mentioned anything about money. Of course, Pastor Rodney blessed me, but there was no guarantee. I had no idea how our ministry would make money. We never discussed how anything would work out, and in the natural, it looked like the economy was about to collapse.

Little did I know that the attendance on the field was much greater than it appeared. Between 11,000 and 13,000 people were watching live online each night. The YouTube videos were reaching over 100,000 views a night, plus it was on television for four hours every night.

I didn't fully understand the impact of *The Stand* until I visited Las Vegas months later. I was in Las Vegas at the Venetian Hotel and Casino, buying Camila something at IT'SUGAR, when a South Korean man approached me and said, "Are you famous pastor from Florida?" I started to tell him he had the wrong guy. Then I thought he might have seen me at The River. I asked him if he saw me on *The Stand* with Dr. Rodney. He told me he and his wife watched every night from South Korea and asked to take a picture with me. That's when I realized I didn't help Pastor Rodney; Pastor Rodney helped me. If I decided not to help Pastor Rodney like he asked because I already had meetings booked and I wasn't sure about preaching on AstroTurf in direct sunlight for hours at a time, it would have been a huge mistake! *The Stand* affected the entire world.

I heard a pastor on Christian television say, "We have authority over coronavirus." That's true, but if I scroll back through his Instagram to March 2020, he wasn't claiming that then. He closed his church for a year and a half during COVID. Anyone can make bold declarations after the danger subsides, but what decisions do you make in the heat of battle?

When I started holding meetings again after preaching at *The Stand* with Pastor Rodney, they were filled with visitors from all over. I would preach at a church that seated 250 people, and 300 people would show up. That one decision changed the course of my ministry.

DECISION 6

MAKING MISTAKES MOVING FORWARD, NOT BACKWARD

Ultimately, if I make any mistakes, I will make them while being aggressive, not careful. I have decided to do what the Bible says, no matter the cost, and I am prepared to deal with the consequences. I have no interest in discovering what happens when you abandon God's Word for safety.

The COVID months were crazy. We broadcasted from 10:00 a.m. until noon. Then, I preached with Pastor Rodney from 7:00 p.m. to 10:30 p.m. and ended each night with *Check the News* from 11:00 p.m. until 1:00 a.m. That was my routine every day. We even broadcasted on Saturdays during the lockdown. That's eight and a half hours of broadcasting each day, not to mention the time we spent in the studio before and after each broadcast. We practically lived there, and we had fun. We were at the office from 9:00 a.m. to 1:00 a.m., but it made the pandemic easy because *we* affected the COVID hysteria and lockdowns instead of sitting at home being affected by them.

I'm thankful to our staff at Revival Today. The pandemic revealed we didn't have any pretend Christians on staff. Not a single person threatened to leave over our lack of masking policies. We set up our control room as a combination gaming den and snack bar. It had a family room atmosphere.

Some ministries discovered their staff was a mixed multitude. I preached at a church where the pastor asked me how I'd like to handle the fact that one associate pastor's wife tested positive for COVID. He didn't respond when I asked him why members of his staff were getting tested for COVID. That's what happens when you hire idiots. We didn't have anyone like that on our staff. Our team stayed strong, focused, and kept moving forward.

 Faith is never a risk; unbelief is a risk.

I gave you a nine-point decision-making process in Part One of this book, but in reviewing these six decisions, I hope it provided a better picture of how they play out in reality. Don't do what's easy; do what's right. The cost of doing what's easy will always be greater than the cost of doing what's right. The cost of doing what's right is paid upfront. The cost of what's easy might be paid three years down the road. It's like putting it on a credit card, but you'll pay it back with high interest. I had to put up with a lot of headaches for three months, but now I'm enjoying life. Other people felt safe for three or six months, and now they're posting #PleaseComeBackToChurch. Whatever risk it seems like you're taking by operating in faith, acting on God's written Word is never a risk. Being out of God's will is what puts you at risk.

AFTERWORD

The Bible is a book about destiny-changing decisions. The woman with the issue of blood decided to travel to Jesus and touch the hem of His garment and was healed. The rich young ruler decided not to listen to Jesus when He told him to sell everything he owned to follow Him. Who knows, maybe we would have been reading about him through the Book of Acts. He might have been an apostle with churches named after him worldwide. But he kept what he had and went down the road.

People aren't judged according to their beliefs; they're judged according to their decisions. The Bible is a book about the consequences of obedience and disobedience to God and His Word. The first four of The Ten Commandments deal with your relationship with God, and the next six deal with your relationship with man. The first four honor God, and the last six honor man.

AFTERWORD

The degree to which you obey God determines your success in life.

> And I saw a great white throne and the one sitting on it. The earth and sky fled from his presence, but they found no place to hide. I saw the dead, both great and small, standing before God's throne. And the books were opened, including the Book of Life. And the dead were judged according to what they had done, as recorded in the books.
>
> — REVELATION 20:11-12

Satan was involved in Adam's loss of the Garden of Eden, but he wasn't ultimately responsible. Satan couldn't do anything until Adam and Eve obeyed what he said instead of what God said. God will not define your life for you, and neither can the Devil define it. Your decisions will define your life.

When faith is tested, it's likened to gold purified by fire. That's how I feel. I don't believe anything differently than I did before COVID started, but now I've proved my faith. You'd have a hard time getting me to worry about anything. I've had several opportunities to back down since then, but I've decided to trust God, and now I see that the Devil's threats are a smokescreen. The Devil doesn't have the power to carry out anything he threatens. I have a different level of boldness I'm sure no one thought was possible.

AFTERWORD

When God said, *"I'll set you far above all nations of the world"* (Deuteronomy 26:19), He meant that if you do what He says, you'll operate above the nation you live in. You'll be able to bring your nation up, but it won't be able to bring you down.

Father, I thank You for every person reading this book. Thank You for bringing them into our lives here at Revival Today. I pray for anything they're going through and any concerns they have. I pray that You'll eradicate those things in Jesus' name. I thank You for them. I give You praise. Thank You for Your presence. Thank You for Your hand that's upon our lives. In Jesus' name, amen.

When he gives an altar call to receive Jesus Christ, my father often says, "God has voted for you, Satan has voted against you. You cast the deciding vote." That's true for more than just salvation. Many Christians decided to receive Jesus at a church service or while watching someone on Christian television. That decision is often made despite a thousand internal voices screaming for you to stay in your seat. But a decision is made when a person does what's right in the face of uncertainty.

This is a book about how your decisions will determine your destiny. No decision will impact your life more than deciding to accept Jesus Christ. Have you made that decision? Can you pinpoint a moment in your life when you committed your life to Jesus Christ? If not, why not do that today—right now?

If you decide today is your day, it's essential to tell others about it. Our friendly staff at Revival Today is delighted to celebrate with you. Please call and speak to someone who genuinely cares about you, will pray with you, and will give you some great tools to help you live the Christian life.

AFTERWORD

"My generation shall be saved!"

— JONATHAN SHUTTLESWORTH

ABOUT THE AUTHOR

Evangelist and Pastor, Jonathan Shuttlesworth, is the founder of Revival Today and Pastor of Revival Today Church, ministries dedicated to reaching lost and hurting people with The Gospel of Jesus Christ.

In fulfilling his calling, Jonathan Shuttlesworth has conducted meetings and open-air crusades throughout North America, India, the Caribbean, and Central and South Africa.

Revival Today Church was launched in 2022 as a soul-winning, Holy Spirit-honoring church that is unapologetic about believing the Bible to bless families and nations.

Each day, thousands of lives around the world are impacted through Revival Today Broadcasting and Revival Today Church, with locations in Pittsburgh, Pennsylvania; Fort Worth, TX; Los Angeles, CA; and Phoenix, AZ.

While methods may change, Revival Today's heartbeat remains for the lost, providing biblical teaching on faith, healing, prosperity, freedom from sin, and living a victorious life.

If you need help or would like to partner with Revival Today to see this generation and nation transformed through The Gospel, follow these links…

www.RevivalToday.com
www.RevivalTodayChurch.com

Get access to our 24/7 network Revival Today Global Broadcast. Download the Revival Today app in your Apple App Store or Google Play Store. Watch live on Apple TV, Roku, Amazon Fire TV, and Android TV.

Call: 412-787-2578

- facebook.com/revivaltoday
- x.com/jdshuttlesworth
- instagram.com/jdshuttlesworth
- youtube.com/@jonathanshuttlesworth

DO SOMETHING TODAY THAT WILL CHANGE YOUR LIFE FOREVER

THUS SAITH THE LORD, **MAKE THIS VALLEY FULL OF DITCHES**. FOR THUS SAITH THE LORD, YE SHALL NOT SEE WIND, NEITHER SHALL YE SEE RAIN; YET THAT VALLEY SHALL BE FILLED WITH WATER... **THIS IS BUT A LIGHT THING IN THE SIGHT OF THE LORD**... AND IT CAME TO PASS... **THE COUNTRY WAS FILLED WITH WATER.**

2 KINGS 3:16-18; 20

Revival is the only answer to the problems of this country - nothing more, nothing less, nothing else.

Thank you for standing with me as a partner with Revival Today. We must see this nation shaken by the power of God.

You cannot ask God to bless you first, prior to giving. God asks you to step out first in your giving - and then He makes it rain. We are believing God for 1,000 people to partner with us monthly at $84. Something everyone can do, but a significant seed that will connect you to the rainmaker.

IF YOU HAVE NOT YET PARTNERED WITH REVIVAL TODAY, JOIN US TODAY!

This year is not your year to dig small ditches. When I grew tired of small meetings and altar calls, I moved forward in faith and God responded. God is the rainmaker, but you must give Him something to fill. It's time for you to move forward! **Will you stand with me today to see the nations of the world shaken by the power of God?**

Revivaltoday.com/give

revivaltoday.com/paypal

Zelle info@revivaltoday.com

 @RTgive

Text "GIVE" to 75767
Call at (412) 787-2578

Mail a check to:

Revival Today P.O. BOX 7
PROSPERITY PA 15329

REVIVAL TODAY Email: info@revivaltoday.com